D0975375

the
art of
the
and how it can
change your life
idea

the
art of
the
and how it can
change your life
idea

John Hunt

Sam Nhlengethwa

powerHouse Books
Brooklyn, NY

To:

Kim, Michael, Luke and Jade.
Inspiration daily delivered.

Thanks:

To Margie Backhouse for planting the seed.
To Sandy Gorgen, Adele Prins, Harry Kalmer and
Sam Nhlengethwa for helping it grow.
To Claude Grunitzky and Emmanuel Andre
for suggesting where it could flourish.
And to all my friends and colleagues,
many of whom orbit TBWA,
for supplying much of the nutriments.

Choose always the way that seems best,
however rough it may be.
Custom will soon render it
easy and agreeable.

PYTHAGORAS

observation
№02

LEMMINGS *have* PLANS too

observation
№01

You get SUNRISE *or*
SUNSET people

observation
№03

IDEAS *have* MOODS

observation
№04

WE are all EQUAL *before* the IDEA

observation
№06

I GOOGLE *therefore*
I am (NOT)

observation
№05

LOGIC *is* KRYPTONITE

observation
№ 10

Embrace DIVERSITY,
it'll HUG *you* back

observation
№ 09

EXPEDIENCY is *not* an IDEA

observation
№ 08

Incremental CHANGE
is fine *if* you're a GLACIER

observation
№ 07

Trust YOUR INSTINCTS,
or they *will* GO AWAY

observation
№ 12

Never put LIPSTICK on a P

observation
№ 11

An IDEA is a PARADIGM SHIFTING
moment that forward projects
FUTURE POTENTIAL in an initially
ETHEREAL *but* progressively
tangible MANNER

observation
№ 13

Think about
the THOUGHT POLICE

observation
№ 14

This just in, *we're* MORTAL

observation
№ 15

Idea APARTHEID is dead

observation
Nº20

It's not the CIRCLE of LIFE,
It's the CIRCUS of LIFE

observation
Nº19

IDEAS *don't* travel well
through a BUREAUCRACY

observation
Nº18

We don't know what we DON'T KNOW *until* we
DO what we don't USUALLY DO

observation
Nº17

Enter the POLITICIAN,
exit the IDEA

observation
Nº16

No one *orders* a bouquet of
BEIGE FLOWERS

inTRODUCTION

I'll admit, to define the arrival of an idea is not easy. Sometimes it just suddenly appears unannounced and sometimes it has to be coaxed with a long line of bread crumbs.

But that's the charm and the challenge of original thought – you start out with no certainty of where you're going to end up. Essentially you're in the pursuit of unexpected relevance. Unexpected might mean the obvious revealed in a new way, but its arrival still surprises. Relevance, of course, is necessary to make an idea useful.

So a new thought is often a tangle of inspiration and a request for it to be reasonable. The problem is, while logic tries to have a mating dance with this swirling dervish everyone gets nervous and walks away. It's just too messy.

This leads to a strange paradox because, at the same time, everyone is noisily yelling that we're moving from the age of information to the age of ideas. Soon, they pontificate, original thinking will be the only currency of value.

Yet, how do most people and organisations welcome the dawn of this golden age? They do exactly what they've done before, hoping that meticulous repetition will somehow allow the light to come through.

Their strategy is clear; the best way to steady a tottering status quo is to cling to it more tightly.

There are many reasons for this reaction. They range from schools that teach us to learn, but not to think, to companies that are actually embarrassed by someone who has a new idea. As if a rash has suddenly appeared in an inappropriate place on the body corporate.

Whatever the cause, the end result is that most people don't understand the nature of "having an idea". Either it's seen as some mystical experience, where a crystal on the forehead might help, or it's confused with incremental change.

All my life, I've only worked with ideas and with other people who were trying to have them. For me, it is an intuitive experience. I love being in a space where a new thought could change the present reality and occasionally even the world.

However, it was only much later that I began to notice a pattern emerge around people and organisations who had ideas and those who didn't.

It seemed strange to me that something as intangible and spontaneous as an idea could have its own universal ebb and flow. I'm also deeply suspicious of rules. However, no matter which part of the world I was in, no matter which nationality I was dealing with, the more I watched, the more the patterns kept emerging.

So, these are my observations. I hope it leads to more people having more ideas more often. I firmly believe it's ideas that prod and push the world forward.

We should all play our part.

Besides, to be successful from now on, having ideas will have to be an organising principle, not just a eureka moment.

You get SUNRISE
or
SUNSET people

I 've never met anyone who doesn't fall into one of these two categories. Everything from family gatherings to boardrooms are dissected by them.

A sunriser gives out energy, a sunsetter sucks it away. A sunriser goes through life open to the idea that the best may still be coming. A sunset person is heavy in the knowledge that the best is past. For him or her, the future is in a calibrated decline: therefore, the present is always sloping downhill.

Age has nothing to do with which category you belong to. Many of the most energising people in the world would be considered "older". The most sunrise person I've ever met had grey hair, walked stiffly and had just spent 28 years in jail.

Nelson Mandela electrified a room, not through soaring rhetoric or slick salesmanship, but through integrity of purpose. He had an idea for a whole country and he wanted everyone to help make it float.

Often in meetings, he'd listen to people being angry about the past. When they were finished, he'd agree with them. They were right, he'd say. But then, he'd ask that their anger at the past not contaminate the future.

When you are angry and right, that's a difficult ask.

But Mandela knew that if he based his idea on the evils of the past, he'd soon have a sunset country.

Sunrise people, like Mandela, also know that if you don't have all the answers yet, it doesn't mean the idea is invalid. Belief has to be the foundation long before the spreadsheets arrive. Sunsetters find any chink in the armour and work tirelessly to make it wider.

It's also important to note that being loud isn't necessarily a distinguishing characteristic of a sunrise person. Increased volume rarely marks you as a fresh thinker. Air is stirred, but little energy is released. The entire essence of the military is to dress people the same and then shout at them a lot. Orders get followed, but not much original thinking happens.

Great ideas often come from quiet people who take stimuli from their surroundings, but work in solitude with their mind.

Irrespective of personality, the clearest signifier of sunsetters, is the amount of mental energy that evaporates when they enter a room. Often, before a word is spoken, you can feel it heading to the exit. It's very difficult to get an idea through them because they don't attack the idea itself, they attack the attitude surrounding it.

> "Let's not get ahead of ourselves."
> "Didn't we try this before?"
> "Which Exco would this report into?"

Sunset people don't kill ideas, they just take away all the oxygen surrounding them.

When Mandela was released, so were a million ideas. Many came to fruition because, at that time, the sunrisers held sway over the sunsetters. It was Spring in the mind of a new nation. And most incredible of all, those ideas joined hands and created a miracle.

LEMMINGS
have PLANS too

We are creatures of habit. And habit can serve its purpose. It's great not to have to stop and think every morning whether your underpants go on before or after your trousers. But habit can also become so deeply ingrained, it produces a mental gridlock. If something new cannot be processed through pre-existing channels, it is rejected.

It's very difficult to get a fresh idea through those addicted to routine. Their thinking grooves have become ruts. They don't see doing the same thing over and over again for a long period of time as habit. They prefer words like *consistency* and *continuity*. They aren't just comfortable with year-on-year sameness, they're proud of it.

The issue often becomes not so much the acceptance of something new, but the ability to let go the old. And this is where the gatekeepers are very crafty.

They present habit as part of their value system.

Just when you thought the idea was through, just as the new initiative is about to happen, the question is asked: Is this really us?

Suddenly the idea is no longer being discussed, but rather the environment in which it finds itself. At this precise moment, habit produces a rearview mirror and begins to vigorously polish it. Nostalgia begins to weave its magic as the good old days are remembered. In a business context, it's usually at this time that the company founder is misquoted and habit is elevated into a sacred right.

It's the reassuring nature of habit that produces its stickiness. It's not an aggressive force. Its power is in its stealth. We can all hide within it. The more the merrier. And whoever is suggesting change is, by definition, the outsider.

The problem with a preset mind, is that it has assumed its way of doing things is best. And habit then proves it so. Habit attracts followers, and the more followers, the stronger the habit. There's great comfort in tracking the footsteps of those in front of you. That way, you don't have to worry where you're going.

I've met many people and companies who are fuelled purely by habit. They are incapable of changing because they are unaware of this. Habit has disguised itself so cunningly, they are totally oblivious to its presence. This is because when change presents itself, habit sends others out to fight its battles. Very few people are prepared to ask themselves: Is there a habit or an idea behind this? Is this the best way or merely the most accepted? These responses inevitably allow fear of the unknown to invite procrastination in, ensuring that nothing happens.

Intellectually, the gatekeepers always say the same thing, "It's still working, so why change?" It's as if the speed of momentum all around them is happily offset by their total lack of movement. They don't realise that changing only when you have to usually means it's too late already. That if you don't anticipate the future, you will be run over by it.

So, like lemmings, they scurry happily, ever closer, to the cliff's edge. And as they follow each other mindlessly into the sea, they still chant, 'Why fix it, if it ain't broke?'

IDEAS *have* MOODS

I deas don't happen in a vacuum. They're sensitive to the environment and often take their cues from the prevailing mood. If you have a room full of scared people, they will tend to give you stiff, small ideas. Fear might be a strong catalyst for entrenching obedience, but it's a lousy motivator for fresh thinking.

An idea can't be bossed into existence. It has to be coaxed into the light. In my experience, that's more likely to happen if the atmosphere is easy and a few smiles are scattered around the room. It's an enigma, but many great ideas happen when you're not trying too hard. Which explains why so many eureka moments occur in the bath or while you're watching your daughter's school play.

However an idea appears, the golden rule is to celebrate, not mourn, its arrival. The fact that it doesn't represent reality as it stands is not only allowable, it's obligatory. Nothing new will happen if it first has to pass some internal sameness test. A vast amount of fresh thinking is stillborn, because the overriding sense is that it's not wanted anyway.

All over the world, at any given moment, someone is calling a meeting under the guise of a "brainstorm". But what they really want is a fine drizzle.

This tentative approach is usually caused by the fact that very few concepts are born perfectly formed and ready to go. So people are scared to float or accept an idea that's not shrink-wrapped in its completeness. It's critical therefore, that, as ideas take their first steps in the real world, they're made to feel welcome. Most of the world's greatest ideas were first very fragile thoughts.

And nothing amputates thinking more completely than early ridicule.

Often the seed of an idea sounds silly, but that's where the originality lies. It just needs time and discussion for it to evolve. What started out as stupidity might not be so dumb after all. Original thinking, taken early, can be moulded endlessly. Bland thoughts can only go where they've been before.

If you allow ideas to germinate a little, you also stand a good chance of them developing their own kinetic energy. Ideas love to bounce off each other. If the mood stays positive, the bounce gets more and more frenetic until it begins to ricochet around your head and around the room.

There is, literally, a surge of energy. Suddenly, everyone has an idea or a piece of one. Everyone starts interrupting. Laughter gets loud. Coffee is gulped. Doughnuts are eaten whole. Pens scribble across pads. Flip charts topple as they're stabbed with markers.

It's intoxicating to be in the middle of all this idea adrenaline. The trick is not to be scared of it. The real value of an idea is to see how far you can push it. It's a legitimate high because it allows your mind and those around you to explore new frontiers. If it gets a little overstretched, there is always time afterwards to pull it back. At the very least, you've shaken the existing boundary ropes. And that feels good.

observation
№04

WE are all EQUAL
before the IDEA

A nyone can have an idea. If we are all supposed to be equal before the law, we are even more equal before the idea. The right to see something from a new perspective belongs to us all. And because it is a personal, internal right we choose to exercise, no one can stop us from doing it.

Even the worst authoritarian governments can't stop you from thinking. Free thought is what they fear above all else. The most banana of republics intuitively know they are just one brave idea away from collapse. Ultimately, they understand they will lose. No army, no torture room, no suitcase stuffed with unmarked bills can help them.

This raw power belongs to everyone. More importantly, the quality of its output does not depend on age, race, gender, nationality, qualification or profession. Sadly though, we always diminish its force by trying to segment its potential. We tend to ask the same people in the same space to come up with something new.

It's not that they're inappropriate, it's just that familiarity tends to breed…well, familiarity. They're hamsters in the same cage; at the very least, they need to be given a new wheel.

Most people and companies have a vast reservoir of fresh thinkers all around them. But they refuse to utilize them because they refuse to cross-pollinate. They choose to believe that we are not all equal before the idea. They don't understand that new perspectives can come from anywhere.

So, no young people are invited to the important meetings about the future of the company. Although they are the future, important meetings belong to the older folks. Corporate behaviour continually reinforces the incredibly stupid notion that the more senior the person, the more prone they are to having big ideas.

Organisations spend perverse amounts of time and energy ensuring that conventional thinking is neatly overlaid with new conventional thinking. They then stand back and tut-tut that nothing new has emerged.

The truth is, we straightjacket ourselves by keeping the potential solution within a certain group. It's human nature to want to work with people we're comfortable with. But we're comfortable with them because they think the same way as we do. To ask this similarity to come up with something that's different is difficult. It rarely happens.

The reality is, the answer lies all round us, beyond the artificial parameters we've given the problem. Most great ideas come from unexpected places, so why don't we open the door to them? All it takes is a very simple mind shift.

Send the word out that ideas have no class system. Juniors can have very senior moments of brilliance – it doesn't matter where fresh thinking comes from, as long as it comes. Encourage cross-border sorties. Mix divisions, business units, age groups and, if possible, countries. Bring in total outsiders and celebrate the fact that they don't think like you.

Disband the politburo and declare an idea democracy.

LOGIC *is* KRYPTONITE

In my mind, I've always seen logic as a solid. It has mass and carries within it a terrifying weight. It is extremely powerful and can stop dreamers dead in their tracks. The problem is, for hundreds of years, we've been taught to respect its potency. There may be many gods, but logic is the Supreme Being.

We all bow at her altar and beg for her blessing. We hang our heads low and whisper supplications because we've been schooled in the belief that if something is not logical, it will not work. If it does not pass the logic test, it is immediately useless and all is lost.

Logic may not be a false god, but we have, at the very least, given her way too much power. Because the opposite of logical is not always illogical. In a given set of circumstances, a thought might not make sense, but if you change those circumstances, suddenly it's watertight.

The critical question to ask is whose logic said an idea will or will not work, and in what set of circumstances was that logic applied. Two hundred years ago, a man might have stuck feathers to his arms and tumbled down a mountainside.

The prevailing logic would probably be fairly strong that nothing heavier than air could fly.

But that hardly gives logic bragging rights for eternity.

Yet, we still give logic this grand sweep whenever someone tries to think, or do, anything new. Logic is the status quo's first line of defence, and is vastly experienced in fighting the most vicious rearguard actions. The reason she is so powerful is she can intimidate with "facts".

More dreams lie crumpled at her feet than before any other obstacle. Millions of individuals and organisations stay unchanged because logic has bullied and embarrassed them into sameness. And that's because, over the centuries, we've allowed its power to cleverly manipulate its importance.

Instead of applying its force at the end of an idea, we've allowed it to be omnipresent at the start. Like a smart-arse heckler at the beginning of the groom's wedding speech, logic deliberately interrupts the flow and makes everyone feel self-conscious.

If logic is introduced too early into an idea, it often kills it. That's because it speaks with history on its side and all its received knowledge can make anything new seem foolish and impractical.

The only way to deal with logic, is to beat it at its own game. Declare that it's illogical to have it around at the beginning of something new. Acknowledge, though, that it does have its place, in the right dosage, at the end of the process. Logic is rarely a catalyst, but it is the consummate filtering process.

Remove her incredible heaviness at the start to ensure the idea floats. Later on, she might be handy to supply a little ballast.

But, keep her in her place.

I GOOGLE
therefore
I am (NOT)

ervation

006

The bugle call of technology gets louder every day. But its rallying call doesn't always bring the cavalry. Some of its notes can be very shrill. And, strangely, nowhere is this more obvious than in the very specific business of trying to create something new.

Of course, nothing has morphed our existence more than the computer chip. The Internet bonds us like superglue. Communication is a predator, high above the clouds, always on the hunt. But in all our getting, sometimes we have got too much.

Information, once a highly prized resource, has, in many instances, now become a commodity. The unintended consequence of this ease of access has been the creation of the data junkie. They are the modern equivalent of snake-oil salesmen. Instead of cajoling from the wheel of their covered wagon, they have a computer snugly hanging from their shoulder strap.

Their pitch is as slick and as rapid-fire as their Power-Point will allow. Bar graphs pirouette delicately with pie charts. Diagrams form and then re-form as if by alchemy.

Colourful type fades on and off with sublime synchronicity. Logos tumble and turn.

It's critical during these types of presentations to reach for the nearest pen and write on your inner forearm: Information, no matter how beautifully it is packaged or re-packaged, does not equal an idea.

Information is nothing more than the raw stuff that might lead you to something new. Having lots of it doesn't make you any cleverer. You can segment it, dimension it or colour-code it if the mood takes you. But until it's seeded with an idea that leads to an action, it's just a lump of words and figures.

The relentless delivery of information dulls the brain and constipates thinking. Those with the thickest files and the most saved documents on their desktops are often those furthest from crisp, clear thinking. Their systems are clogged.

This is a worldwide problem of massive proportions be-cause we have chosen to confuse volume with substance. We have become slaves to information, yet what we really need is insight. Insight is the high fibre we get from information and 90 percent of the time, the immediate precursor to an idea.

Billions of words have been written on the inaccessibility of fresh water in many developing countries. Reports on the issue are piled skyscraper high. Yet, it needed the insight that, because of the vast distance needed to travel to collect water, this had often become the children's chore. This, in turn, lead to the idea that a merry-go-round can sometimes be the answer. Simply reconvert the time and energy of these children into fun.

Now, in a number of villages all over the world, the spinning of a playground favourite, ideally next to a school, acts as the pump mechanism for transporting water many miles away.

Insight appears when you look for meaning rather than facts.

Insight demands that you use your brain actively. The passive accumulation of data won't help you here. And those who merely reshuffle and repackage know the report they leave behind is thick with information because it is thin on insight.

We do ourselves a disservice by believing we know more because we have more "stuff". Information can camouflage as much as it can illuminate. Likewise, organising data is not an end in itself. Just as numbering a set of pages doesn't add to their content.

It takes a restless mind to dissect what is recorded so the insight can be found. An inquisitive brain soon sees through the scam. Most information is dross masquerading as knowledge. And most of this knowledge is static and academic anyway. Ideas don't come from existing facts, but from the holes we drill through them.

observation
N⁰07

Trust YOUR
INSTINCTS,
or they *will*
GO AWAY

In an age where everyone seeks certainty, reference power, measurement and research, instinct sounds like a concept that belongs to a bygone era. It's too difficult to define. Too primordial. Besides, universities don't run courses for it. Over time, the word has been repositioned to mean the opposite of intellectual. If you are instinctive, you are somehow part animal and in the sophisticated human world, that's bad.

So, the first question at the job interview is never, "Do you think you have good instincts?" Instead, you are asked about your training; questioned on what you are qualified to do. The interviewer is looking for the certainty of your learning and the quality and depth to which it is ingrained in you.

Of course, a good education is not a bad thing. But it seems to come at a terrible cost. Higher education usually has the unhappy knack of planing off the rougher edges of instinct. To listen to your inner voice, to take a chance, to believe because the feeling says so, is just too flaky.

Why listen to millions of years of evolutionary honing, when you can run the numbers again and let them tell you what to do?

Fewer and fewer people pay any attention to what their gut is trying to tell them. They shun this feeling because it is exactly that...a feeling. And feelings are messier than facts. They're difficult to matrix, quantify or extrapolate across a spreadsheet. So they're disregarded altogether.

Yet, when you're desperate for an idea, it's the most precious commodity on earth. At the early stages of something new, that's often all you've got. An instinct, an inner twitch in your gut, that says you might be on to something big.

Way before a thought can evolve into something we believe in, it floats in the primitive soup of instinct. Those who come up with the best ideas are those who are comfortable with the fact that, sometimes, you just know before you know why.

Sadly, we have been taught that the exact opposite is true. The *why* is not allowed to slowly mature. If reason cannot be immediately articulated, you're forced into the corner and told to wear the dunce's hat.

Nothing is more depressing than being in a room with people who have had their instincts beaten out of them. They look at you with the doleful eyes of neutered cats.

observation
№08

Incremental
CHANGE
is fine *if*
you're a
GLACIER

It's probably a combination of the world's relentless momentum and our extreme interconnectedness that makes tiny step changes less and less relevant. Especially if those changes don't occur on a daily basis. Adapting slowly, in most cases, is now the equivalent of staying the same – or worse.

We think we've changed, we think we've moved forward, but the backdrop we're operating against has moved even quicker. We stop to check our bearings, flushed with the speed of our progress, and find we're further behind than before.

That's why ideas are so important; they're the only mechanism we have to keep up.

But it's equally important to understand that ideas have trajectories and that they move to the expectancy level you put around them. Therefore it's critical to aim high. No matter the context, an idea needs a decent arc. It needs to leap out of the present sameness and clearly carry everyone who's following it to the other side.

And, even with an original thought wrapped tightly in your head, it's tough to leap an abyss in two bounds.

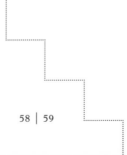

A huge amount of breakthrough thinking doesn't make it, not because the idea is wrong, but because, at the crucial moment, our courage leaves us. We notice how high we are and we look down. Suddenly we wonder whether the big leap is the right strategy and consider a game of triple jump. And shouldn't three jumps be cut into more manageable portions of six?

Soon the idea is inching along and, unable to maintain impetus, it plummets.

The problem with incrementalism isn't just its lack of velocity; it's that it ends up performing the function of a dying black hole. It draws smaller and smaller amounts of energy into itself and then disappears altogether.

A small, gradual idea tends to disappear the moment you've just had it because there's not enough concentrated energy to take it anywhere. Why put so much effort into something that will change things so marginally?

I've attended hundreds of meetings that adjourn with the unstated consensus to do nothing. The idea is minuted, agreed upon and dead. It will die by ping-pong e-mails and a dwindling attendance at follow-up meetings. For a while, everyone is copied on everything to record that no one is doing anything. Eventually, the idea implodes and quietly evaporates in cyberspace.

If the idea has a powerful curve to its trajectory, the opposite is true. What was moribund and lifeless, begins to have a pulse. Others add turbo-boosters to the original idea. Instead of nose-diving, the arc grows longer and stronger.

Everyone wants a piece of the action, not just so they can claim part ownership, but because contribution to original thinking also gives a sense of mission. The measurement of baby-step progress releases no sense of purpose. It confirms our averageness.

Big ideas have a "what if" quality about them that initially defies measurement and metrics. And that's a good thing. All that can, and will, come later. But much of the attraction and fascination around a big idea is that it can't immediately be quantified. Nothing motivates people more than being told they have permission to let their imagination out of its cage. To stretch the arc of an idea. What the hell, maybe even do a loop-de-loop.

If you're going to leap, you might as well quantum leap.

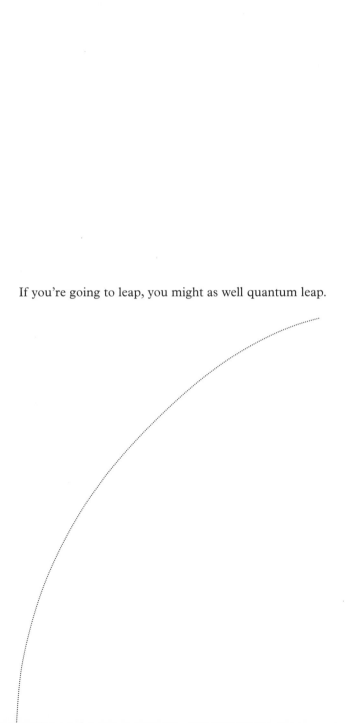

observation
№09

EXPEDIENCY
is *not*
an IDEA

observation

N.º09

It's difficult to have an idea in an environment that stands for nothing. The quality of the idea is never discussed, but rather how much the implementation could upset those surrounding it. Everyone applauds the thinking while simultaneously creating an escape hatch for themselves concerning the execution.

New thinking usually needs the involvement of others; this often leads to the debate about how difficult "they" are. The suggestion is made that the idea be toned down a little so "they" might find it more palatable. Maybe it should be held back for six months until "they" are in a better frame of mind.

Very few ideas survive the third person trap.

If you're not careful, expediency quickly dusts everything. In this world Romeo and Juliet would have to skip excitedly into the sunset, because most people like happy endings.

Taking the path of least resistance is the surest way to celebrate what you've already achieved and stay a slave to the ordinary. Expediency is so handy because the more you use it, the more it sounds like good, old-fashioned common sense.

Besides, you've got the courage – it's the other guys you're worried about. "They" just don't get it.

Expediency wins so often because the obvious is overlooked. If a new idea is worth anything, it should make everyone a little nervous. It will be tougher to sell. But these are all good signs. It means the idea carries change within it. And part of our makeup as a species is to push back hard before we accept anything new.

The problem comes when that push-back is used as an excuse to perpetually defer doing anything new. It's what "they" want. Fresh thinking needs a champion and a group with guts surrounding it. The opposite of expediency is tenacity. The first test of an idea is the level of commitment to it.

"They" aren't the problem. Others will embrace and celebrate the new even more if they can sense the courage it took to get there.

And although this runs counter to much conventional wisdom and business practice, I've never seen an idea brown-nosed to greatness.

Expediency is so liberally applied because of its ability to offend no one. It allows you to take three steps forward, then three steps backward, and congratulate all those concerned on the progress made. In-the-moment expediency is your friend. Meetings are less tense and everyone leaves claiming they're comfortable.

In the longer term, though, expediency is extremely corrosive to ideas. It allows you to marinate in the mediocre. Everyone is content, but no one is ecstatic. The more you use it, the more it offers a false sense of security. Why change? Everything seems okay.

But, if you stay middle of the road, you will eventually be run over both ways. The middle ground is always the most dangerous place to be. No man's land is not safe territory.

Unfortunately, it soon becomes obvious that if you stand for nothing, then that's also what you attract. For ideas to work, they have to bounce off something of substance. If they are just walked through one compromise after another, they lose their power.

When things are going well, taking no risks seems like a very smart strategy. When times are tough, though, you'll notice expediency, which is meant to create all those happy, smiley faces, is suddenly wearing a smirk.

Embrace DIVERSITY,
it'll HUG *you* back

I f you want something new to emerge, you want people in the room who don't think like you. This might seem obvious, but for most, in practice, it's counterintuitive. The person tasked with finding a new way forward immediately calls a team of mini-me's to the table.

They are "me's" because the prerequisite is that they think the same as their team leader, and "mini" because said leader has ensured that everyone attending is more junior. That way, no one is confused as to who the boss is. The first ten minutes of these meetings are fairly animated. The scope of the problem is discussed as pens tap chins in excited anticipation.

Thereafter, the terrible impact of intellectual incest becomes more and more apparent. Everyone is agreeing with everyone, but nothing is actually happening. There are no sparks being caused by the happy friction of two people tackling an idea from opposing angles. Instead, sameness and sameness are playing footsie-footsie together, and you know whatever they're going to produce is not going to be pretty.

It's not just excruciatingly dull, it's also unnecessary.

The advantages of embracing diversity are immediate and tangible. Walk into a room with a true mixture of people and you can feel a different kind of energy. The meeting hasn't even started, yet the differences, whether it's accents or dress sense, have already had an effect. It's a more interesting place to be. Minds automatically open as they adjust to absorb new stimuli.

Many people are scared of diversity because they think it's somehow the opposite of *teamness*. This is a fallacy. In searching for a fresh idea, the best teams I've worked with have been the most diverse. By channelling our differences at a problem, something richer seems to appear. Besides, these days, ideas can go global in a nanosecond, so originality has to be peppered from all sides. More and more, I've found that genius is in the collective as much as it's in the individual.

But that collective should be eclectic and not an excuse to join an intellectual country club.

Working with people of different backgrounds doesn't just give the group a different point of view, it makes you reassess your own. This is extremely powerful because we're all trapped in what we've previously learnt. And "previously learnt", often means what we've previously been told. And that's often not true or entirely accurate.

Usually our thinking ends up in a cul-de-sac because of the assumptions we've made along the way. Once someone from a different space tells you these assumptions aren't necessarily true, it's much easier to reroute yourself to an idea. We need others to take our blinders off, mainly because we don't realise we're wearing any.

The moment diversity isn't seen as conflicting views, but rather as multi-source intelligence, things begin to happen fast. Everyone knows they can be exactly who they are, as they contribute to change. The ability to create fresh impetus, to find something brand new, increases exponentially. The richer the mix the richer the outcome, guaranteed.

Many dabble in diversity-lite. They pay lip service to using difference and smugly feel they are being politically correct. This is superficial, destructive and misses the whole point. They claim that too much diversity dilutes existing culture and values. In my experience, the exact opposite is true.

Besides, it's much easier to create something new if your building blocks are different. Playing with existing sameness is a game of diminishing returns. Letting people in who see the world differently creates a unique alchemy. Diversity doesn't want an air kiss, it's waiting for a tight squeeze.

You'll be happily surprised with what happens next.

An IDEA is a
PARADIGM SHIFTING
moment that forward projects
FUTURE POTENTIAL
in an initially ETHEREAL
but progressively
tangible MANNER

B eware the faux intellectual.

Pretend intellectualism is the Dark Lord of fresh thinking. This kind of person does not want to have new ideas. He wants to discuss them. At length. For him, debate and argument aren't a means to an end, they are the end.

A faux intellectual wouldn't know an idea if he sat on one, but quickly recognises a thought that, in discussion, could make him look smart. He packages his thinking as if addressing a debating society and relishes the chance to ask himself questions.

This internal examination of his own brilliance can be fairly time-consuming. A pattern emerges where he perpetually answers his own questions and presumes all those listening are riveted by the dialogue. Everyone, of course, is invited to participate, but find themselves stopped mid-sentence with phrases like, "I think what you're trying to say is...."

If there are two faux intellectuals in the room, you double your chance of failure and extend the time of the meeting proportionately. Within seconds they go about tidying each other into opposite corners. For them, the highest form of embarrassment is to agree with anyone.

They guarantee this won't happen by ensuring the discussion goes wider and wider. The further you move from the original purpose of the debate, the more space you have to exploit differences of opinion. The fact that it's irrelevant doesn't matter because it all sounds so intelligent.

The meeting started off looking for an idea on how to sell more socks and suddenly you're arguing whether *Australopithecus robustus* was the earliest form of biped to have toes.

Faux intellectuals are the Anti-Idea because original thinking comes from making a complicated thing simple and not the other way around. Thinking has to be funnelled, not dispersed. All great ideas bounce off a very deep basic understanding, and not the frilly bits that surround it.

It's also incorrect to assume those who articulate the best, have the smarter thinking. Ideas aren't necessarily word based. They appear first, and then need to pass through a language filter to be communicated. I've met many people who are stunning thinkers but poor speakers. The onus is on us to listen to the idea and not the words.

Words can be very beautiful or extremely dangerous. They can focus our thinking with laser-beam clarity, or dull the brain with endless gobbledegook. Usually, there's just too many of them. Discussion is vital, but after talking "about", you also need to think "through".

Silence is the perfect place for an idea to grow in.

After hours of debating the same issue, I find the best dialogue happens when no one says anything.

Although everyone's thoughts are private, a group consciousness hovers in the room that somehow connects everyone. Once the talking starts again, there's nearly always consensus.

Understanding, beyond words, has produced an idea.

It's obvious: an original thought has no need or knowledge of clever wordplay or intricate discussions on the nuances of semantics. A heated debate is worthless if the idea attached to it stays cold.

Never
put LIPSTICK
on a PIG

observation
№ 12

I f something is fundamentally bad or wrong, it's pointless trying to embroider it with good ideas. If the premise is false, no amount of great thinking is going to change that. Yet time and time again, ideas are asked to fight lost causes.

The slaughter is as predictable as it is bloody.

Although this is patently a useless exercise, it is employed endlessly all around the world by just about everybody. The reason is pretty transparent; it's much easier to ask for "new ideas" than it is to change what is systemically incorrect. It also shifts the target away from the real problem to all those lousy ideas surrounding it.

There must have been thousands of meetings and millions of man-hours spent trying to improve apartheid. Yet, strangely enough, not one of those ideas ever scored a ten out of ten.

Ideas can only reach their full potential when the context they're operating in is honest and open. Smart people find the skeletons in the closet almost immediately. Thinking usually starts with interrogating what's already there; you can't suddenly close doors and say certain rooms are off-limits.

When this happens, the process becomes corrupt. A meeting is called because ideas are needed for a new launch that's not selling. Some brave individual says maybe they should start with the product itself. It's inferior and needs improving. This does not make him insightful in the eyes of his peers, this makes him a smart-ass.

His colleagues tell him that they know the product is inferior – that's why they need a really terrific idea.

Once the dice have begun to roll this way, it's almost impossible to stop. No matter how flimsy the idea is, it becomes consumed by its own self-importance. There is little or no foundation of integrity, so the process begins to bloat with hype. Having determined that there is nothing of genuine value to say, the strategy is to proclaim this as loudly as possible. The hope is that the increased decibel level will somehow change behaviour.

When this doesn't work, it is dishonest to claim that the idea failed.

As the world gets more competitive and shrill in its desperate attempt to attract people's attention, hype is being confused more and more with an idea. Hype can be memorable, even extraordinary in the moment, but it's not built to last. By its very nature, it must evaporate as the next blast of buzz appears.

Yet, more and more people with less and less to say are turning to it as an alternative to doing the hard yards. Instead of packaging a smart idea so it can become more successful, the packaging itself becomes the idea. It's like throwing newspaper onto a fire. You have a brief moment of pyrotechnics and then you're left with nothing.

The truth is, a large number of hopeless situations get perfumed with ideas because those who caused the hopeless situation aren't the ones asked to come up with the ideas. These are the toughest meetings. Everyone knows the basic premise is a crock, but no one is allowed to say so.

I was once invited to an "idea session" where the first paper handed out was a list of all the things we weren't allowed to discuss. It's not easy trying to fly when your wings have been clipped. More importantly, these sessions lead to deformed thinking. If you're not allowed to discuss the essence of the problem, any idea generated is just a form of mental propaganda.

There is no greater demotivation than calling a group of people together and then telling them what and where they must think. The good news is, the exact opposite is also true. The rewards of an honest discussion can be beyond measure.

Think
about the
THOUGHT
POLICE

E very group, every family, every organisation has its equivalent of the Thought Police. These people are the high priests of conventional wisdom. Their minds live to articulate what *is*, in such a manner as to confirm what *shall be*.

And there is no more powerful righteousness than self-righteousness.

Although their knowledge is meant to fuel our present-day activities, they tend to often use the past tense.

Even recent history is full of myth and legend and is therefore a very powerful place to choose to live. Time bestows upon it a sense of the sacred. It's also very difficult to argue with what has been, especially if you weren't there. The wisdom of the past always seems deeper rooted than the still-ricocheting ideas of the present.

Some members of the Thought Police see themselves merely as a kind of walking archive, a perpetual source of reference. Others are more aggressive. They have a mission. They believe experience has revealed the holy tablets of the future. Past successes should be codified into a set of rules and their job is to make these rules scripture.

These Thought Policemen aren't necessarily malicious, though they do always feel that change is somehow disrespectful to what has already been created. Any twist on convention is viewed with suspicion and seen as devaluing existing practice rather than improving it. The same question is always asked: If this new way is better, why isn't everyone else doing it?

Conventional wisdom borrows continually from habit to puff up its point of view. This allows it to present itself not only as correct, but as having been ratified as so. The protectors of conventional wisdom are well organised and battle hardened. Their fortress is ringed with a moat of logic, and experience peers out from every turret. They have survived many sieges before. You may be able to catapult an idea over their massively thick walls, but that's the last time you'll see it alive.

The drawbridge stays up.

It's extremely difficult to crash the defences of the Thought Police with a fresh idea. That's because much of their argument is perfectly valid. And, of course, there are many lessons you can learn from the past. New ideas aren't always good ones and change can bring periods of instability and uncertainty.

The problem isn't conventional wisdom itself, but the fact that the Thought Police have elevated it to the Holy Grail. Yet, they never asked themselves the obvious question. If the existing idea is so powerful, why does it need to be protected with all those walls? Thinking gets stronger the more it is exposed – it shouldn't become a prisoner to its own handlers.

When any group turns conventional wisdom into a cult, it's almost impossible to thread an idea through them. Some of the most articulate people I've ever met are Thought Police. They have a blinding passion to guard what is, at the huge detriment of what might be. This is always made more difficult if they've previously been successful. Any idea that doesn't come from the old place is discarded immediately. The idea is seen as irrelevant and even a little dishonourable.

It's tough to explain to them that an idea can start out as original but not stay that way. Or that it was so good everyone started to copy it. Or that time alone can nudge initial brilliance into conventional wisdom.

Which is why those manning the battlements should pause and think hard. When the walls finally do come crashing down, they'll find what they thought they were protecting is long gone anyway.

This just in,
we're MORTAL

observation
№ 14

Ideas are like humans: their life spans are not infinite. A few, like the wheel, change the world and last for centuries. Others, like bell-bottom trousers, have a lesser impact. The point is, the germination of an idea is a function of the circumstances at a very particular moment in time.

And as time moves on, the validity of that idea is always being put to the test.

No thinking, no matter how incredible, is frozen in time and judged against a static background. Just because the wheel was such a breakthrough, doesn't mean it has to stay in stone or wood. Some ideas are so fundamental and powerful they are reincarnated year after year. Others are destined to bloom for a few months and then die.

The trick is to know which is which. I've attended a few meetings where an idea, clearly alive and kicking, has had the last rites administered to it. More often though, I've watched exhausted and comatose thinking being wired up to life support.

Sometimes it is a genuinely close call, but generally we dig our heels in for the wrong reason. Even the best blacksmith in town eventually gets run over by the horseless carriage.

It helps to accept that the life cycle of an idea is determined by a vast range of interventions. Some are frivolous (like fashion), others are more weighty (like the environment). Either way, there's not much you can do about it. The original thought has to adapt to remain relevant or it should be allowed to die a natural death. Ideas are as Darwinian as life itself – only the strongest survive.

It also needs to be accepted that change is refusing to take its foot off the accelerator pedal. This means ideas have to be born quicker if they're going to expire that way too. While this is no excuse to be perpetually winging it, procrastination doesn't serve much purpose either. Thinking without a sense of urgency rarely sees the light of day.

Although we all complain about not having enough time, speed, properly managed, can be your friend. A group of people in a room with too little time are more productive than a group with too much. Ideas respond well to a closed door and a deadline.

Over time, relentless pressure will take its toll, but it's a far better option than endless navel gazing. A tight time frame creates focus. If an idea is told it has to appear on Wednesday, miraculously it usually does. If its given a six-month gestation period, then that's what it'll take.

Ideas can sense the surrounding heat. If there is no immediate need, brains become lazy. Thinking moves to a more academic mode. We ponder. It's all very therapeutic and philosophical and, at certain times, very necessary, but it's not the shortest line to an idea.

If it's understood that ideas, like other perishable products, have a sell-by date, then speed is not your enemy, but rather your modus operandi. Thinking doesn't have to have long loops from one person to the other. At the beginning of the process, the closer everyone is physically, the better. E-mails

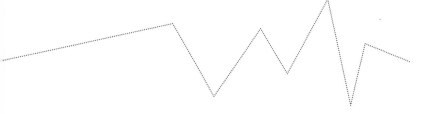

and telephone calls tend to dissipate the magic. Even if the thought is clearly articulated, it's not attached to the mood. And an idea in its early stages, without the positive atmosphere around it, is tough to float.

Those not in the initial meeting often feel cheated. Worse, the more enthusiastic everyone is, the more cheated they feel. Those who attended the meeting end up being defensive as they explain how excited everyone is. It's the same fruitless task as explaining why a joke is funny. They nod, they get it – but no one laughs.

If everyone is in the same room though, a hothouse effect is created. Most problems can be short-circuited, and the growth of ideas is enormously stimulated. The level of thinking is not only higher, it's also faster. Spontaneity has a place to live because it doesn't have to be translated.

Speed to market is determined by how quickly a group of minds can dance in unison. And, these days, no matter how ethereal the creation of an idea might be, it also has to be punctual.

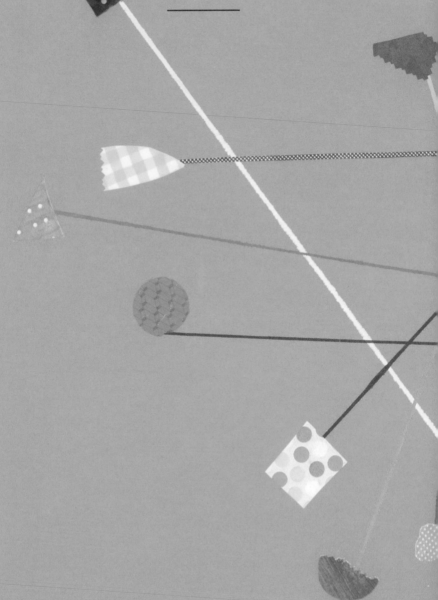

observation
№ 15

Idea APARTHEID is dead

All the lines are blurring. Categories can no longer be rigidly classified. Ideas hop from one to the other, shamelessly borrowing from everywhere. Everything is at an intersection with something else. You can be a specialist at what you do, but you better have damn good peripheral vision at the same time.

A deep dive into a specific category often reveals less about its future than an understanding of the broader context it's playing in. An idea in the category "Sport" might be good or bad depending where the categories "Entertainment" and "Media" are going. Ideas no longer live solitary existences.

Genius is nearly always the outside view looking in; the clever coupling of two or more seemingly disparate things. Of course, looking from within is an option. The gradual improvement of what has always been done works if where you're playing stays the same. But change doesn't keep regular hours. Sticking to the knitting doesn't mean obsessively refusing to look at what's going on around you.

Best-in-class irrelevancy isn't much of a prize.

Original thinking needs a longer leash. Continuously taking your mind for a walk to exactly the same place doesn't really exercise it. You can't connect different things together if what you're seeing is always the same. It's because you know the narrow confines of your particular space that you have to venture further afield. The gap between what you already know and what you're exploring is often where the best ideas pop up.

Scouting laterally to find ideas that already exist and then retooling them isn't intellectual plagiarism, it's how the world works. That's the path newness often chooses to take. It's not only legitimate; it might be the only way to survive. If a bookstore is going out of business, buying better books might not help as much as installing a cappuccino machine. If that idea came from the coffee shop around the corner, well, so be it.

Often, an idea is route-marched to a new place by necessity. It might still be the best in the category, but that's little comfort if the category is shrinking. This forces even the most myopic thinker to search beyond his normal demarcated zone. Here cross-pollination can take place, and that vastly increases the chance of a sturdy hybrid emerging.

If you're not borrowing from the world, you're building a house to hubris. No idea is so perfect that it can feed off itself forever. And hubris is the next idea's easiest and most favourite target. It's like a face waiting to be slapped. It's always when an idea is category king and convinced of its immortality that two seemingly disconnected thoughts, usually from the wrong side of town, happily join.

This new union doesn't just reset the category, it often obliterates it.

It's not rational, but I've often seen ideas stopped in their tracks because they've been deemed to come from the incorrect place. They are not purebred. Instead of understanding the endless pattern of connections, some believe thinking is preserved by imprisoning it in its existing, neatly labelled box. As if where a thought comes from is more important than where it's going to.

It might work for wine, but being anal about the provenance of an idea is incredibly stupid and guaranteed to stunt any new perspectives.

The excuse usually offered is a need for focus. But focus that's so narrowly defined can only lead to the skinniest of solutions, which won't last for long. In the end, a relevancy check has to be done, but you should still start with the funnel to your mind being as wide as possible. That way, you can go hiking, discover your pants are covered in burrs and invent Velcro.

No one *orders*
a bouquet of
BEIGE FLOWERS

I deas aren't fussy about where you have them, but that doesn't mean you have to make it harder for yourself. History is full of the *bonanza* thought arriving in offices that are garages and on desks that are packing crates. Hollywood always reminds us that staring at peeling wallpaper from your mattress on the floor, while desperation sucks at your soul, often produces the goods. But once survival mode has been transcended and there's food on the table, things tend to change a little.

Suddenly, having an idea, or getting others to have them, is merely part of the business grind. Some energetic individual claps his hands and asks everyone to "think like an entrepreneur" and to "pretend this is your company". Although asked just to "bring your imagination", employees automatically open their desk drawers as if expecting to find it nestling between their stapler and their reserve stash of paper clips.

Suitably motivated, this group now shuffles down the office corridor with all the spontaneity of *Dead Man Walking*. It's not going to help that the meeting room they're headed to has brown walls, no windows and chairs designed for those who prefer to stand. The cause is further hobbled if this is the same room where, in the previous week, management announced how its layoff and wage freeze policy was actually good for everybody.

Sometimes the reasons are tangible and sometimes not – either way, certain spaces are better than others at helping produce ideas.

It's smarter to take the walking dead past the brown meeting room, into the lift and up to the roof garden of the building. Even if there's no roof garden. Sitting on an air vent while you watch the janitor's laundry flapping in the breeze, is more conducive to original thinking than staring at a crooked flip chart in a faceless meeting room.

Change the physical space you're in and your brain follows suit. I've noticed, in an absolutely literal sense, if you give people a distant horizon, their ideas are less short-term. If you're physically on top of the world, it's more difficult to think small, mean thoughts. A point of view is sometimes just exactly that. And by altering it, an enormous amount of stimuli is allowed in.

While it's obvious that one of the easiest ways to kick-start the brain is by changing the real world that surrounds it, this is rarely done. Instead, ideas are relentlessly demanded from endless rows of glass cubicles or from the sea of an insipid open plan. It's difficult to find inspiration when the colour scheme of the average workplace is variations of oatmeal and the only part of the environment that talks back to you is the automated coffee machine.

That said, it's unlikely many organisations will invest in a Zen garden or appoint a feng shui master to the board. And, as pleasant as a daily massage and aromatherapy is, there is a fine line between taking your mind to an idea and taking it for a holiday. However, you don't have to go to extremes to make your surroundings work for you.

If you can't change the room, change the room. Play a piece of music at the start of the meeting. Turn the pictures upside down and see if anyone notices. Ask everyone to bring in their favourite quote and pin them on the wall. Spend ten minutes with the lights switched off and think in the dark. Released from the four walls, ideas float everywhere. Sometimes to places you're a little embarrassed about.

Whether through schooling, habit or plain laziness, our thinking develops a thick crust of sameness. By changing

our environment, even momentarily, the space we operate in becomes a powerful ally in cracking that sediment.

At the very least, go for a walk. Feel the rain or the sun on your face. Listen to your footsteps and watch your shadow. The space you return to might be the same, but you'll be different.

observation
№ 17

Enter the
POLITICIAN,
exit

the IDEA

observation

№ 17

N othing slices an idea to shreds quicker than the serrated edge of politics. Trying to chase original thinking down a Machiavellian blind alley is a total waste of time. A low level of politics always exists when you're trying to sell your point of view, but the introduction of a predator politician takes this to a new dimension. This is because he has no interest in the quality of the idea, other than how it will enhance his personal agenda.

Often that means killing everyone else's thoughts, or diluting them and thereby claiming ownership. This is particularly prevalent if he is one of the more senior people around the table. Politicians are not keen to bask in reflected glory. They'd prefer you to understand that they are at the centre of the idea solar system. All light radiates from within them.

They have a stunningly simple technique to achieve this. The summation. The politician will take the idea everyone else has come up with and feed it back to them as if it were his own. If the broad thought suits his needs, only minor changes will appear. If it's counter to his specific agenda, it's slowly strangled with twisted logic.

Besides performing assassinations at the wrap-up stage, politicians puncture the clarity of purpose needed to solve the problem at hand. A certain amount of childlike naivety is invaluable to open the mind. This is difficult with a hidden agenda smiling at you from across the room.

The problem is further compounded by expert politicians initially being able to keep their ulterior motives secret. This drives the rest of the room crazy as they try to navigate around something they're not sure is there. Suddenly finding a compelling idea is no longer the goal; instead, everyone tries to outsmart the politician. This is almost impossible.

The mind of a predator politician is wired differently. If he feels he's losing to his colleagues, he just changes sides. He starts agreeing with them, sometimes even taking the lead. This gives him the credibility to plan the death of the idea after the meeting. If you know where it's going, you know where to ambush it later.

I don't think there's much you can do with a serial politician. Their behaviour is pathological. The results of any discussion concerning his conduct lasts as long as he thinks it's important for you to think he's reformed. The truth will out, though: although politicians can be devious in the extreme, self-interest always breaks camouflage.

It might be difficult to articulate someone else's hidden agenda, but it's impossible not to feel it. It sits in the room as if it has a chair of its own. Smiles that are too wide and laughter that's too loud merely add to its presence. No one is fooled.

Unfortunately, self-interest can be a group enterprise as well, especially as having an idea is turning more and more into a team sport. So, it's critical not to turn the process into a political rally. Tough debate is essential and it's fine to have different candidates support different thoughts. The problem arises when votes are cast for reasons that have nothing to do with the validity of the idea.

To see the result of days of hard work clog itself up in block voting is madness, but it happens all the time. The debate then further descends into a weird form of pork barrelling. Pieces of the idea are conditionally approved based on trade-offs that have nothing to do with the original purpose of the meeting.

Ideas have to be judged at their highest level, where they can do the greatest good. The tunnel vision of an individual or a special interest group makes innovative thinking unrecognisable and usually meaningless. It is said that politics is the art of the possible, and that may be true, but having an idea is the art of the impossible. You have to dream and then make real something that did not previously exist.

The very last thing you need is a politician obscuring your sight line.

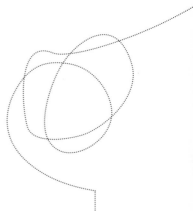

We don't know
what we
DON'T KNOW
until

we DO
what we don't
USUALLY DO

observation
№18

observation
Nº 18

I cdnuol't blveiee taht I cluod aulacity uesdnatnrd waht I was rdanieg. The phaonmneal pweor of the hmuan mnid, aoccdrnig to rscheearch at Cmabrigde Uinervtisy, mnaes taht it dseno't mtaetr in waht oerdr the ltteres in a wrod are, the olny iproamtnt tihng is taht the frsit and lsat ltteer be in the rghit pclae. The rset can be a toatl mses and you can sitll raed it whotuit a pboerlm. Tihs is bcuseae the huamn mnid deos not raed ervey lteter by istlef, but the wrod as a wlohe. Azanmig, huh? Yaeh, and I awlyas tghuhot slpeling was ipmorantt!

Until the previous paragraph was sent to me by a friend, I didn't know my mind was capable of reading words if only the first and last letters were correct. This realisation only came about because I was open to try it when the opportunity presented itself.

It's extremely liberating and honest to admit that we know very little about almost everything. This is not to make us feel small and insignificant, but rather to make us feel excited about how much we still have to learn. How we view this fact determines our ability to think in new and creative ways. In the literal and figurative sense, it's not only the glass that's either half full or half empty, it's also our brains.

The tired and the negative see the contents of their cranium as a passive instrument with a dwindling capability. The energetic optimist actively rearranges this storage facility to increase its capacity. And the easiest way of achieving this is to do things you don't normally do.

Just going on holiday is an obvious demonstration of this. Most people return from their vacations with a more open and energetic view of life. They have broken the normal

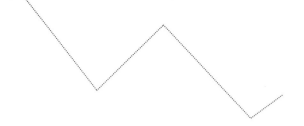

patterns of their existence. But you don't have to leave the country or your job to actively rearrange the building blocks in your brain.

The easiest way to make the mind zigzag is to keep feeding it the unusual. And the world's not short of material. If you love watching motor sport on TV, next time try watching it set to classical music. High-powered cars spinning out of control and smashing into each other to Handel's *Water Music* offers the mind fresh gymnastics. Even just going for that new dish in a restaurant reorders the impulses dancing around inside your head. It says you're still open for business of the untried kind.

The fact that our playground is so infinite is to be celebrated. Its vast scope shouldn't make us fearful. We add to the stretch of our brain the more we stimulate it. Experimentation with the unknown is not something to be contained and watched with a beady eye. In the land of ideas, a comfort zone is not an environmentally friendly place to be.

More importantly, actively breaking conformity-creep keeps you battle ready. As much as we want to push and pull our thinking to some lightbulb moment, the truth is, often an idea just reveals itself. That revelation is nothing more than an accumulation of all the fresh stimuli that's been allowed to collect. By keeping your mind fertile, even the tiniest seed of a thought has a good chance of growing into something extraordinary.

On the other hand, fear of the unknown plagues the imagination in the same way it brought dread to ancient mariners. If you're worried about falling off the end of the earth, your thinking stays close to shore. Unfortunately, in this instance age, again, doesn't always bring wisdom. Tales of sea monsters from old hands don't do much to boost confidence.

Yet the greatest ideas often tumble from the most rigid truths that are proved to be incorrect. An open mind in a closed world is where the densest originality is found. It's no easy task though. There's a huge need for courage and persistence, and a willingness to forgo instant gratification. It's only once you've circumnavigated the world that everyone starts believing it might not be flat.

IDEAS *don't*
travel well through a
BUREAUCRACY

T he high mortality rate of ideas often has less to do with their quality and more to do with their mode of transport. This is because most people believe that fresh thinking, like a sack of potatoes, can follow the standard distribution process. Occasionally a "Fragile: Handle with Care" sticker might be attached, but the usual organisational flow takes it from there.

Bureaucrats take special delight in torturing anything new. They feel that is what they are paid to do. As they stick sharpened bamboo poles into sensitive parts, the shrieks of pain merely confirm a job well done. Bureaucrats believe allowing newness in is an abomination to all they hold true, and that passing that newness on unscathed is the most heinous of all crimes.

This is further complicated by a bypass strategy very rarely working. Bureaucrats are wily folk. In the short term you can win the battle, but they nearly always win the war. An idea might be a little more difficult to run to ground than monthly expense reports, but they'll get you anyway.

It's incorrect to think that bureaucracy only exists in the finance or procurement department. It's at its thickest when any idea crosses any border. The moment a new thought leaves its home base, it's viewed with suspicion. That suspicion takes the form of a filter, and that filter, if not carefully managed, turns into bureaucracy. The integrity of an idea can't be honestly interrogated if it's surrounded by resentment because it came from somewhere else.

It's correct and essential to question everything, but when that questioning leads to ever widening circles of endless debate, the game is over. Layers of decision-making institutionalise procrastination and often elevate it to an art form. It might be meticulously and precisely recorded, but that doesn't change the fact that it's a waste of time.

If fresh thinking is to stay fresh, it has to be quickly accepted, rejected or positively modified. Refusing to send it anywhere because of where it came from is criminal. And parking it in some distant way station helps no one.

I now strongly believe ownership is much less important than portability. Even if it's "your" idea, the smartest thing to do is hand it over immediately and declare it "their" idea. Only the most massive of egomaniacs won't concede that it's now "our" idea.

This doesn't make it an orphan. The idea now has many mothers and fathers. By worrying less about its parentage, you also acknowledge that it might grow in different ways than first imagined. By openly letting others contribute and have a point of view, you allow more stimuli into the process. This also remains true to the natural order of idea-mobility. A caged thought can't fly. Creativity, or the power of our imagination, has always been a two-act play. First there's the ah-ha moment, then there's the power of it as it radiates out.

That power won't percolate very far, especially through a bureaucracy, if those around the idea feel they are just bystanders. You might get a rubber stamp and a tick-in-the-box, but, mysteriously, the power is often diminished. The idea has been noted, but that doesn't mean it has been adopted. If, however, ownership can be conferred on everyone, the miraculous begins to happen. The idea turns into a movement.

And the world rallies behind a cause, not an instruction.

The moment it's understood that the idea belongs to everyone, any fresh input adds to its momentum. Even better, the bureaucracy manning the idea border patrol no longer asks you to unpack everything each time you cross. The goods in transit belong to them as well. It sounds paradoxical, but because the idea is now better understood, it's also easier to direct. Control has a lighter touch because feedback is naturally built in.

Many believe participation is another word for chaos and prefer to keep their clammy hands directly on the levers of power. This might be appropriate for owners of sweatshops, but it's not an intelligent option for the transportation of new thinking. "My" idea has to be force-fed, and, in my experience, has four degrees of separation before it's diluted to the point of uselessness. "My" idea is still practised in companies, countries and families with dictatorial tendencies, but isn't sustainable in the long run. In the end, even the greatest concept needs the ripple effect to keep it going and the community of others to keep it fresh.

Besides moving an idea along by its own weight, anything allowed to grow open-source reminds us that it's everyone's job to be curious. It'll also soon prove you can't over-estimate the knock-out effect of a moment's originality that's about to travel well.

It's not the
CIRCLE of LIFE,
It's the CIRCUS
of LIFE

observation
№20

T he cold truth is, we may be bored with a life that moves in a straight line, but we cling to the comfort it brings. Much of our existence is in the slack of knowing what we'd like to do and the lack of courage to do it. Usually this fear is rooted in the need for change to present itself in a neat, orderly fashion. We want the future to be revealed in sequential bite-size chunks that are easily digestible.

Unfortunately the world doesn't operate that way and pretending it does creates the perfect killing field for ideas. Reality is an unpredictable set of leaps and jerks that happen faster and faster. Fresh thinking is the only saddle we have to ride the unknown, so we might as well get used to making it up as we go along. It also helps if we start enjoying that ride.

Enthusiasm, provided it's not confused with hype, allows a change in direction to be a source of adventure rather than panic. Ambiguity doesn't have to equal confusion. Sometimes it pays to revel in the options as you go about pruning them. Acknowledging that tomorrow is too tight a corner to see around keeps everyone sharp and nimble. Certainty is just a superficial examination of the future.

Ideas often shrivel because we're scared the environment we're putting them in will change. And it most certainly will. But if you're not in that space, you have no way of affecting it. An idea in play can morph and adapt to new circumstances – waiting for everything to be perfect before joining the game will take an eternity.

The smartest ideas come from those who've learnt to surf the unpredictable and the unexpected. Sure, they get dumped occasionally, but that's no excuse to get out of the water. In a strange way, perpetual change brings its own rewards. You can be serene in the knowledge that while looking right, you will be smacked from the left. The time to be truly nervous is when things keep going exactly to plan.

The big trick is to be relaxed about uncertainty and, if possible, to even enjoy it. An idea can wriggle through almost anything, but the shuttered grid of an uptight mind is a particular challenge. It's difficult to have an epiphany if all you want revealed is what you already know.

I've found it often helps to put your normal self to one side while being roller-coastered to a new thought. Experience, though invaluable in one sense, also has the horrible habit of closing the mind down. After a certain age, many people feel obliged to have ideas in sepia. This can be avoided by temporarily becoming someone else. It certainly helps with the whiplash.

The less-clogged find it easy to do this via their imagination; to move momentarily to a parallel universe. Others need a little help from a prop or two. The simple act of putting a hat on can lead to an immediate transformation. The hat becomes a symbol of the other person you can become. This altered state of consciousness gives you permission to take your mind somewhere else and think from an entirely different perspective. It can also make the most reserved personality relax because it's that funny guy in the hat coming up with those crazy ideas, not him.

I once gave a staid banker a Mickey Mouse hat and asked him what changes Walt Disney would've made if he owned the bank. Half an hour later he sang all his ideas, each one to a different tune from *The Lion King*. This was no superficial karaoke moment. It brought the realisation that his institution had entirely neglected to talk to young teenagers. He just needed to become one to fully understand that.

It's a pity, and counterproductive, that being playful is corporately frowned upon and not seen as appropriate in the business environment. Initially, more than anything, ideas need to be surrounded by a lightness and a little childlike wonder. Having a sense of humour shouldn't be a punishable offence. Court jesters see the world the wrong way around and that's often the best angle to let the truth in.

Whatever the portal to an idea is, we can only look for clues in the surrounding patterns. The moment we demand rules, the opening begins to close.

In the end it's an individual quest. We have to find our angles of inspiration in our own way. We know they exist, we just have to learn how to call on them.

Not knowing in advance exactly how the call will be answered, shouldn't halt the journey. The fact that we start out not sure of where we're going is what makes the quest so noble. There's a little Don Quixote in all original ideas. It's just those windmills are in our minds and we should never be scared to tilt at them.

JOHN HUNT

John Hunt is an award-winning playwright and author, as well as Worldwide Creative Director of TBWA.

Keen to celebrate all forms of creativity, he cofounded globally-renowned TBWA\Hunt\Lascaris with the mantra, "Life's too short to be mediocre".

In 1993, John was intimately involved in Nelson Mandela's election campaign. Although rather harrowing at the time, this unique moment in history ushered a battered South Africa into the warm light of democracy.

In April 2003, John moved to TBWA's New York headquarters to assume the role of Worldwide Creative Director. There he helped reshape the network to celebrate original thinking and ground-breaking ideas. In 2008, both *Adweek* and *Ad Age* named TBWA, Agency of the Year.

John has since returned to South Africa, where he continues his Worldwide role.

SAM NHLENGETHWA

Sam Nhlengethwa is a collagist, painter and jazz fanatic. He once said, "Painting jazz allows me to literally put colour onto those vocal chords". He is one of Africa's most influential artists.

After being named South Africa's Young Artist of the Year in 1994, Sam quickly gathered global recognition. His work has been shown at the National Museum of African Art, D.C.; Whitechapel Gallery, London; and was reproduced in *The 20th Century Art Book* (Phaidon Press, 1996).

From humble beginnings, Sam's talent, although forged during the apartheid years, has always reflected a calm celebration of the human spirit. Perhaps because Sam is so painfully aware of the past, his work acknowledges not just who we are, but also what we can become. This is also probably why his originality lacks all pretension.

the art of the idea

and how it can change your life

Compilation and Editing © 2009 powerHouse Cultural Entertainment, Inc.
Text © 2009 John Hunt
Illustrations © 2009 Sam Nhlengethwa

All rights reserved. No part of this book may be reproduced in any manner in any media, or transmitted by any means whatsoever, electronic or mechanical (including photocopy, film or video recording, Internet posting, or any other information storage and retrieval system), without the prior written permission of the publisher.

Published in the United States by powerHouse Books,
a division of powerHouse Cultural Entertainment, Inc.
37 Main Street, Brooklyn, NY 11201-1021
telephone 212 604 9074, fax 212 366 5247
e-mail: artoftheidea@powerHouseBooks.com
website: www.powerHouseBooks.com

First edition, 2009

Library of Congress Control Number: 2009932101

Hardcover ISBN 978-1-57687-516-2

Printing and binding through Asia Pacific Offset, Inc., NY
Art direction and design by Adele Prins, www.prinsdesign.co.za
Photography of artworks and portraits by John Hodgkiss

A complete catalog of powerHouse Books and Limited Editions
is available upon request; please call, write, or visit our website.

10 9 8 7 6 5 4 3 2

Printed and bound in China